T0199198

AuthorHouse™
1663 Liberty Drive
Bloomington, IN 47403
www.authorhouse.com
Phone: 1 (800) 839-8640

Because of the dynamic nature of the Internet, any web addresses or links contained in this book may have changed since publication and may no longer be valid. The views expressed in this work are solely those of the author and do not necessarily reflect the views of the publisher, and the publisher hereby disclaims any responsibility for them.

Any people depicted in stock imagery provided by Getty Images are models,
and such images are being used for illustrative purposes only.
Certain stock imagery © Getty Images.

This book is printed on acid-free paper.

ISBN: 978-1-7283-2826-3 (sc)
ISBN: 978-1-7283-2825-6 (e)

Library of Congress Control Number: 2019914656

Print information available on the last page.

Published by AuthorHouse 09/20/2019

authorHOUSE®

Hi! My name is Jackson and I am seven years old.
This is my wheelchair.

Have you ever had your preschooler point to someone in the mall and ask loudly, "Why is that man so fat?" or "Why is that little girl in a wheelchair?" or "Why does that little boy look funny?" If you answered yes to any of these, you know how important it is to teach tolerance and acceptance at this very young age. Thus, this book is written for preschoolers to introduce them to a sweet little boy with multiple handicaps, who just happens to like the same things that they do.

It is my hope that by having an adult read this book to them, they will learn that people are the same on the inside, in spite of their mental challenges or physical differences. It should be a fun read that parents or teachers can use to stimulate young minds to ask questions and encourage empathy for their peers.

I am different than you because I can't walk or talk or do things the same way you do But we are the same, too. I like to listen to music and read stories with my little brother, Luca, just like you.

On some mornings, Luca and I go to school. We eat breakfast and watch cartoons before we leave. I like Peppa Pig and Paw Patrol. Do you like cartoons, too?

My class is different because some of my friends are in wheelchairs, too. But it is the same when we sing and draw and have snacks, just like you. I laugh and giggle when my friends make the puppets talk to me!

Then, when Luca and I come home, I like to eat lunch, just like you. I have special food in a tube that someone in my family feeds me. Luca has pasta and likes to taste my vanilla milk. I think you would like it too!

After our naps, Mommy puts me in my special stander. It helps to make my legs stronger. I don't like it very much. But she puts soft animals on my tray and I listen when Elmo talks.

And sometimes, I have to do my exercises with my special toys. It is very hard for me to use my hands, but I like it when I can make the music play.

If it is a nice day, we take a walk outside and go to the ice cream store. I love to feel the sun and breeze on my face. I like ice cream, just like you! Daddy puts it on my lips so I can taste it. Vanilla is the best! What flavor do you like?

Just like you, I visit my grandparents. Nonno and Nonna have a big garden and lots of toys for Luca and me. It is so much fun! Then Daddy and Mommy and Aunt Cindy and Uncle Dana come and we all eat dinner. Everyone talks to me and plays with me and gives me hugs and kisses. Maybe your grandma and grandpa hug you too!

15

When we go to Nanny and Poppy's house they hug me too! Nanny sings to me, and Poppy plays ball with Luca. We all go on walks around the neighborhood or we go to the library and the park.

Nanny always gets special books to read to my brother and me. Then we play at the park and Poppy puts me in the special swing. Luca runs and jumps and is very fast!

I like to see my aunties too, just like you. They come to visit us every week. They play with me and make me laugh and we all exercise. I love it when Daddy does his push-ups over me and kisses me every time! Do you like to exercise, too?

But most days we have family time. When Daddy and Mommy come home, we have dinner. It is very busy then. Mommy feeds me and Daddy gives me my medicine every night. After dinner, we sometimes play our instruments and pretend we are in a band. Or we all read or build with our blocks. I hold some and someone helps me put them together.

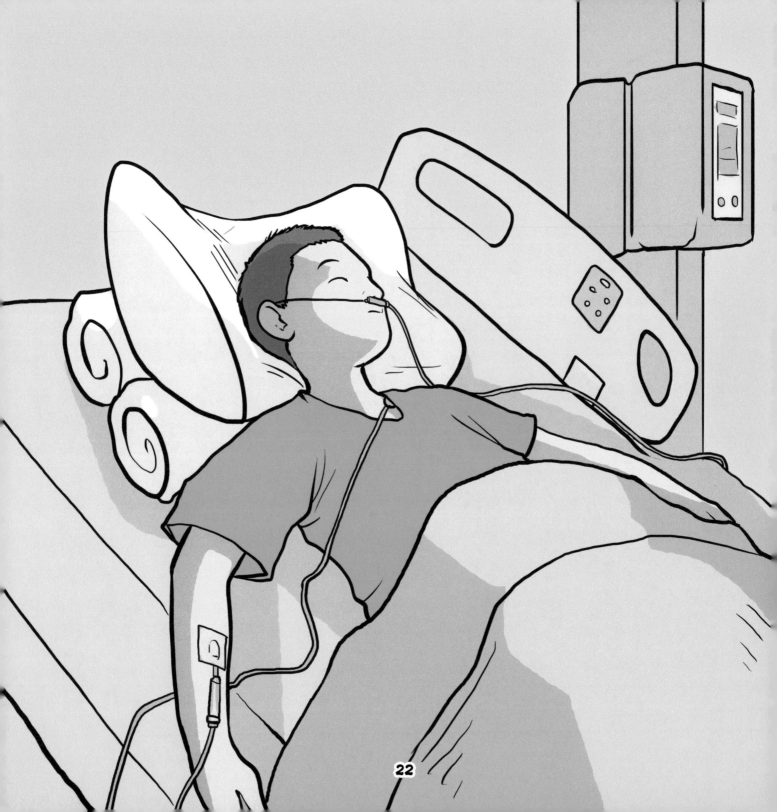

But, not everything is the same. Because I have special needs, I take lots of medicine every day to help me be strong. And I have special machines to help me breathe at night. When I get really sick, I have to go to the hospital for a few days. The doctors and nurses and my Mommy and Daddy take good care of me. And there are musicians who come and sing to me and play the guitar. Except for going home with my family, that is the best part!

So now you know that we are different, but the same. We both like music and toys and books and ice cream and hugs and kisses and especially being with our families. I hope I get to meet you one day so we can be friends! Love, Jackson

As an educator, mother and grandmother to a special needs child, Dr. Andrea Vanzant wanted to explain to young children that their classmate, while different, still enjoyed many of the same things that they did. With a doctorate in Curriculum and Instruction and thirty years of teaching experience, she has written this book for pre-school children to help them accept others and include them in their daily activities. It is also a testament to the power of love in the extended family of a special needs child.

Printed in the United States
By Bookmasters